Data Injection Overview :

Data lake : A data lake is centralised storage repository used to store large amounts of structured,semi-structured and unstructured data. It has can have different formats of data like log files, click stream, social media IoT devices.

Data Lake Vs Data Warehouse :

Data Lake	Data Warehouse
It can be structured,semi-structured and unstructured	Data organised into single schema; like tabular formats used in RDBMS
Any data that may or may not be curated (i.e. raw data)	Highly curated data that serves as the central version of the truth
Low cost	Expensive storage that has faster response times.
Data scientist and data developer	Business analysts
Machine Learning, predictive analytical and data discovery	Batch reporting,BI, and visualisation

Data Injection -

1. Big data Injection involves transferring of data, especially unstructured data,from where it originated,into a system where it can be stored and analyse such as Hadoop.
2. The injection process can be continuous or asynchronous, real time real time   Or both, depending upon the characteristics of the source of origination.
3. In scenario where the source and destination do not have the same data format or protocol,data transformation or conversion is done to make data usable by the destination system.

Data Injection Tools -

Choosing data injection tool is important which in-turn based on the factor like data source , target and transformation.
Apache Sqoop , Apache Kafka, Apache Flume
Data injection tools provide user with a data injection framework that makes it easier to extract data

from different types of sources and support the range of data transport protocols.

Data injection tools also eliminate the need for manually coding individual data pipelines for every data source and accelerate data processing by helping you deliver data efficiency to ETL .

Apache Sqoop -

Sqoop, an Apache Hadoop ecosystem project is command line interface application for transferring data between relational databases and Hadoop. It supports incremental loads of a single table or a free from SQL query. Imports can also be used to populate tables in HIVE or HBASE. Exports can be used to put data from Hadoop into a relational database.

Sqoop is Apache Hadoop Ecosystem project whose responsibility is to import or export operations across relational databases.

The reason for using Sqoop are as follows :

1. SQL server are developed worldwide .

2. Nightly processing is done on SQL server.
3. Sqoop allows to move certain parts of data from traditional SQL database to Hadoop.
4. Sqoop transfer data effectively and swiftly.
5. Sqoop handles large data through ecosystem.
6. Sqoop brings process data from Hadoop to the application.

Sqoop is required when a database is imported from a Relational Database (RDB) to Hadoop or vice versa.

- **While exporting database from RDB to Hadoop :** User must consider the consistency of data, consumption or production system resource, and preparation of data for provisioning that data to downstream pipeline.
- **While importing data from Hadoop to RDB :** User must keep in mind that directing accessing data residing in external system

within a MapReduce framework, complicates applications. It exposes the production system to excessive load originating from cluster node.

Benefits of Sqoop -

1. Transfer data from Hadoop to RDB and vice versa.
2. Transforms data in Hadoop with MapReduce or HIVE without extra coding.
3. Import data from RDB to the Hadoop Distributed File System (HDFS)
4. Exports data back to RDB.

Sqoop Processing -

The processing of Sqoop cam be summerized as follows:

1. It run in a Hadoop Cluster.
2. It imports data from RDB or NoSQL DB to Hadoop.
3. It has access to Hadoop core,which helps in using mapper to slice the incoming data into unstructured formats and place the data in HDFS.
4. It exports data back into the RDB, ensuring that the

schema of the data in the database is maintained.

Sqoop Execution Process -

- The dataset being transferred is divided into partitions.
- A map-only job is launched with individual mappers responsible for transferring a slice of dataset.
- Each record of the data is handled in a type-safe manner.

Importing database using Sqoop -

$ sqoop import - -connect jdbc:mysql:/ localhost/ database name (goes here) - - username (what you have set) - - password (what you have set) - - table (name of table which you will be processing will go here after table)

Sqoop Import process -

- Gathering of Metadata : Sqoop introspect the database to gather the necessary metadata for the data being imported .

- Job summitted to cluster :
  A map - only Hadoop job is
  submitted to the cluster of
  sqoop
- Data is transferred : The
  map only job performs data
  transfer using the metadata
  captured.

The imported data is saved in the
directory on HDFS based on the
table being imported . User can :

1. Specify any alternative
   directory where the file
   should be populated.
2. Override the formate in
   which the data is copied by
   explicitly specifying the
   field separator and
   recording terminator
   character.
3. Import data in Avro data
   format by specifying the
   option , as -avrodatafile,
   with the import command.
4. Sqoop supports different
   data formats for importing
   data and provides several
   options for tuning the
   import operation.

**Exporting the data from
Hadoop Using Sqoop -**

$ sqoop export - - connect jdbc:mysql :// localhost/database name goes here - - username (as set by you) - - password (as set by you) - - export -dir / data /sqoop/export output/ part -0000 (this will be your directory where you are exporting data) - - table (table which you want to export) - - input field terminated-by '\t'

- Perform the following steps to export data from the Hadoop using sqoop :

- Introspect the database for the metadata and transfer the data.
- Transfer data from HDFS to DB.
- Sqoop divides he input dataset into splits.
- Sqoop user individual map task to push the splits to the database.
- Each map task perform this transfer over many transactions to ensure the optimal throughput and minimal resource utilization.

Sqoop Connectors -

The different types of sqoop connectors are :

- Generic JDBC connector -> Used to connect to any database that is accessible through JDBC.
- Default Sqoop Connector -> Designed for the specific database such as MySQL ,PostgresSQL, Oracle,SQL Server and DB2.
- First-Path connector -> Specializes in using specific batch tools to transfer data with high throughput.

Controlling Parallelism -

- By default sqoop typically import data using four parallel tasks called mappers.
- Increasing the numbers of the task might improve import speed.
- You can influence the number of tasks using the - m or - -num-mappers option.

$sqoop import - -connect jdbc:mysql ://localhost/(you database name goes here) - - username (what you have set) - -

password (what you have set) - -
table (table name goes here) -m 8

Limitations of Sqoop -

- Client side architecture does import some limitations in sqoop:
- Clint must have JDBC driver installed for connectivity with RDBMS.
- It requires connectivity to cluster from client .
- User has to specify username and password.
- It is difficult to integrate s CLI within the external application.
- Sqoop is not best supported with NOSQL DB because it is tightly coupled with JDBC semantics.

Apache Flume -

Apache Flume is the distributed and reliable service for effectively collecting, aggregating, and moving large amount of data into Hadoop Distributed File System (HDFS).

It has simple and flexible architecture which is robust and fault-tolerant, based on streaming data flows.

Components

- Log data
- Web server
- Source-> Sink-> Channel
- HDFS

Source consume the event deliver to it by the external source like web server .When flume source receives an event it stores it into one or more channels . The channel is the passive store that keep the event until it is consumed by flume sink. The sink removes the event from the channels and puts its into an external repository such as HDFS or forwards to a next flume agent .

Why Flume -

Flume is helpful in business scenario like :

A company has thousands of services running on different server cluster that produces many large data; these log should be analysed together.

Problem : The current issue involves determining how to send the logs to setup that has Hadoop.The channel or method used for sending process must be reliable, scalable, extensive and manageable

Solution : To solve this problem log aggregation tool called Flume can be used. Apache Sqoop and Flume are the tools that are used to gather data from different sources and load them in HDFS. Sqoop in Hadoop is used to extract data from database like Teradata, Oracle, and so on, where Flume in Hadoop sources data that is stored in different sources, and deals with unstructured data.

Flume Model -

Agent : Agent is responsible for receiving data from the application. Running flume agents insure data is injected in Hadoop.

- Source - Tail Apache HTTPD logs
- Sink - Downstream processor node.

Processor : Process are responsible to process intermediate processing of these jobs

- Source : Tail Apache HTTPD logs.
- Decorator : Extracts browser name from log string and attaches it to the event.

- Sink : Downstream Processor node.

Collector : Collector is responsible for writing these data to the permanent HDFS storage.

- Source - Tail Apache HTTPD logs
- Sink - Downstream processor node.

Flume Goals -

1. Ensuring reliability by processing tunable failure recovery modes.
2. Attain extensibility y using plug-in architecture for extending modules.
3. Achieve a scalable data path that can be used to from a topology of agents.
4. Create manageability by centralising a data flow management interface.

Extensibility in Flume -

- It is a distributed and partitioned messaging system.

- Flume can be extended by adding Sources and Sinks to existing storage layers or data platforms.
- General Source include data from files, says log, and standard output from any linux process.
- General Sinks includes files on the local Filesystem or HDFS.
- Developer can write their own Sources or Sinks.

Scalability in Flume -
Flume has horizontally scalable data path which helps in achieving load balance in case of higher load in production environment.

Common Flume Data Source -

- Sensor Data
- Status Updates
- Network Sockets
- Social Media Post
- Program Output
- UNIX Syslog
- Log Files

Flume Data Flow : Syslog -> Flume Agent (Source, Channel, Sink) -> Hadoop Cluster
Syslog Server
|

Source(Syslog) —->Channel (Memory)—->Sink (HDFS)

|
HADOOP
CLUSTER
Components in Flume
Architecture :

- Source - Receives events from the external actor that generates them.
- Sink - Sends an event to destination and stores the data into centralised stores like HDFS and HBASE.
- Channel - Buffer events from the source until they are drained by the sink and acts as a bride between sources and sinks.
- Agent - Java process that configures and hosts the source,channel and sink.

Flume Source :

- Netcat - Listens on a given port and turns each line of text to event.
- Kafka - Receives events as message from Kafka topic.

- Syslog - Captures message from UNIX Syslog daemon over the network.
- Spooldir - Used to ingesting data by placing files to be ingested into "spooling" directory on disk.

Flume Sinks :

- Null - Discard all events received (Flume equivalent of/ Dev/ null)
- HBASE - Stores event in HBASE
- HDFS - Writes event to file in specified directory in HDFS .

Flume Channels :
Important for buffering input speed to output speed.

- Memory :

Stores events in machines RAM.
Extremely fast but not reliable as memory is volatile .

- Files :

Stores events in machines local disk.

Slower than RAM but more reliable as data is written to disk .

- Memory :

Stores events in database table like jdbc.
Slower than file channel .
Flume Agent Configuration File :
#Define sources, sinks, and channel for agent named 'agent1'
agents.sources = mysource
agent1.sinks = mysink
agent1.channels = mychannel
#sets a property 'foo' for the source associated with agent1
agent1.sources.mysource.foo = bar
#sets a property 'baz' for the sink associated with agent1
agent1.sinks.mysink.baz = bat
Flume : Sample Use Cases :
Flume can be used for a variety of use cases:

1. To collect logs from nodes in Hadoop cluster.
2. To collect logs from services such as http and mail.
3. To process monitoring.
4. To collect impressions from custom applications for an advertisement network.

Apache Kafka -

Kafka is high performance, real time messaging system. It is an open source tool is the part of Apache project.

The characteristics of Kafka are :

- It is a distributed and partitioned messaging system.
- It is highly fault tolerant.
- It is highly scalable.
- It can process and send millions of messages per second to several receivers.

Kafka can be used for various purposes in the organisation, such as:

- Messaging service : Kafka can be used to send and receive millions of messages in real time .
- Real-time stream processing : Kafka can be used to process a continuous stream of information in real time and pass it to stream processing system such as Storm.
- Long Aggregation : Kafka can be used to collect physical log files from

multiple system and store them in central location such as HDFS .

- Commit log service : Kafka can be used as an external commit log for distributed system.
- Event sourcing: Kafka Can be used to maintain a time-ordered sequence of events.
- Website activity tracking : Kafka can be used to process real-time website activity such as page views, searches, or other actions users may take.

Aggregating User Activity Using Kafka -

Kafka can be use to aggregate user activity data such as click, navigation, and searches from different websites of an organisation; such user activity can be send to a real time monitoring system for offline processing.

Customer Portal 1	Customer portal 2

Kafka Cluster

Real time monitoring system	Hadoop offline processing

Kafka Data Model :

The Kafka Data model consist of messages and topics .
Messages represents information such as lines in a log file, a row of stock market data , or an error message.
The process that serves within the Kafka is known as Broker.
A Kafka consist the set of Broker that process messages.

Kafka Architecture :

- **Topic :**
- A topic is a category of messages in a Kafka .
- A topic is divided into one of more partition which consist of ordered set of messages.
- Kafka provides the Kafka-topics.sh command to create and modify the topic.
- **Partitions :**
- Topics are divided into partitions which are the unit of Parallelism in Kafka.
- Partitions allow messages in topic to be distributed to multiple servers.
- A topic can have any number of partitions.
- Each partitions should fit single Kafka server.

- The number of partitions given decides the parallelism of the topic.

Partitions Distribution :

- Partitions can be distributed across the Kafka cluster.
- Each Kafka cluster can handle one ore more partition.
- A partition can be replicated several servers for fault-tolerance.
- One server is always marked as leader for partition and the others are marked as followers.
- Leader controls the read and write for partition,(-m) whereas, followers replicate the data.
- If a leader should fails,one of the followers automatically becomes leader.
- Zookeeper is used in leader process selection.

Producers :

- The producer is the creator of message in Kafka.

- The producer will create the message by placing it into particular topic.
- The producer also decide which partition to place message into.
- Topic should already exist before a message is placed by producer.
- Messages are added at one end of partitions allowing to use first in first out (FIFO) algorithm.

The producer side APIs provides interface to connect to the cluster and insert messages into a topic.
Step to setup Producer Side API :

1. **Get a handle to a producer connection.**

- Each consumer belong to consumer group.
- A consumer group may have one or more consumer.
- A consumer specify what topics they want to listen to.

- A message is sent to all the consumers in the consumer group.
- A consumer group is used to control the actual messaging system .

Step to setup Producer Side API :

- **Set up a producer configuration.**

Properties props = new Properties ( );

props.put("metadata.broker.list", "localhost :9092");
props.put("serializer.class", "Kafka.serializer.StringEncoder");
ProducerConfig config = new ProducerConfig(props);

- **Get a handle to a producer connection.**

Producer<String,String>producer = new producer <String, String>(config);

- **Create message as key and value pairs.**

```
String key1 = "first",String
message1 = "This is first
            message";
String key1 = "first",String
message1 = "This is first
            message";
```

- **Submit the message to a particular topic.**

```
String topic ="test";
KeyedMessage<String,String
>data = new
KeyedMessage<String,Strin
g>(topic,key1,message1);
producer.send(data);
KeyedMessage<String,String
>(topic,key2,message2);
producer.send(data);
```

- **Close the connection.**

```
producer.close( );
```

- By default, a message is submitted to a particular partition of the topic based on the hash value of the key. A programmer can override it with the custom partitioner.

Consumer :

- Once we have produce the messages the consumer becomes the receiver of that messages in Kafka.
- Each consumer belong to consumer group.
- A consumer group may have one or more consumer.
- A consumer specify what topics they want to listen to.
- A message is sent to all the consumers in the consumer group.
- A consumer group is used to control the actual messaging system .

Step to setup Producer Side API :

- **Set up consumer configuration.**

```
Properties props = new
       Properties ( );
props.put("zookeeper.connect",
    "localhost :2181");
   props.put("group.id",
      "mygroup");
ConsumerConfig config = new
   ConsumerConfig(props);
```

- **Get a handle to the consumer connection.**

```
ConsumerConnector consumer;
consumer =
kafka.consumer.Consumer.createJ
avaConsumerConnector(config);
```

- **Get a stream of messages for a topic.**

```
String topic = "test";
Map<String,Integer>
topicCountMap = new
HashMap<String,Integer>( );
topicCountMap.put(topic, new
Integer(1));
```

```
Map<String,List<KafkaStream<b
yte[ ],byte [ ] >>>
consumerMap
=consumer.createMessageStreams
(topicCountMap);
List<KafkaStream<byte[ ],
byte[ ]>>streams =
consumerMap.get(topic);
```

- **Loop over message and process them.**

```
for (final KafkaStream
stream : streams) {
```

```
ConsumerIterator<byte[ ],
byte [ ]> it = stream.iterator(
);
while(it.hasNext( ))
System.out.println(new
String(it.next( ).message( )));
}
```

- Close the connection.

consumer.shutdown( );

- Message can be read from a particular partition or from all the partitions.

Kafka Connect :
Kafka connect is a frame work for connecting Kafka with external systems such as databases, key-value stores, search's indexes, and file system, using connectors.

Confluent Connector :
Confluent connector is an alternative to Kafka Connect which comes with some additional tools and clients, compared to plain Kafka and some additional pre-built connector. Such as -

- Kafka Connect JDBC
- Kafka Connect S3
- SAP Hana Connector

www.ingramcontent.com/pod-product-compliance
Lightning Source LLC
LaVergne TN
LVHW072052060326
832903LV00054B/418